The New York SPORTS WIZ Trivia Quiz

by John Murphy

Red-Letter Press, Inc.

THE NEW YORK SPORTS WIZ TRIVIA QUIZ
Copyright ©2000 Red-Letter Press, Inc.
ISBN: 0-940462-93-1
All Rights Reserved
Printed in the United States of America

For information address:

Red-Letter Press, Inc.
P.O. Box 393, Saddle River, NJ 07458

ACKNOWLEDGMENTS

Cover design
and typography: s.w.artz, inc.

Editorial: Ellen Fischbein

Contributors: Angela Demers
and Jack Kreismer

INTRODUCTION

Red-Letter Press proudly steps up to the plate with *The New York Sports Wiz Trivia Quiz*. Formatted in ten-question quizzes, it features an all-star selection of stumpers on the Big Apple's sports beat.

John Murphy brings you a book loaded with local trivia ... Who was the first player in baseball history to have his number retired? ... At what event was the largest Giants Stadium crowd ever? ... Who played with basketball's Knicks and baseball's White Sox?*

Now let's find out if you're a New York sports nut or not. Let the quizzes begin.

Jack Kreismer

Publisher

*The answers are: Lou Gehrig ... a mass celebrated by Pope John Paul II ... Dave DeBusschere.

FIRST DANCE

The following players were known primarily for playing with New York teams but actually began their careers with other cities. Match the player with the city.

1. Dave DeBusschere		a)	Baltimore
2. Keith Hernandez		b)	Boston
3. Roger Maris		c)	Chicago
4. Mark Messier		d)	Cleveland
5. Earl Monroe		e)	Detroit
6. Graig Nettles		f)	Houston
7. Charles Oakley		g)	Indianapolis
8. Babe Ruth		h)	Minneapolis
9. John Starks		i)	San Francisco
10. Rusty Staub		j)	St. Louis

ANSWERS

1. E
2. J
3. D
4. G
5. A
6. H
7. E
8. B
9. I (for the Golden State Warriors).
10. F

Sec.	Row	Seat	Enter Gate B
82	E	17	

"So I'm ugly. I never saw anyone hit with his face."

–Yogi Berra

1998
NEW YORK, NEW YORK

While Frank Sinatra belted out the song, the year was all
New York, as in Yankees. Here's a quiz about that club.

1. Including the regular season, playoffs, and World Series, how
   many games did they win ?

2. What teams did the Yanks beat in the post-season?

3. In what stadium(s) did they play their home games?

4. What former Met and Yankee pitcher did the Yankees beat
   in the post-season?

5. What Yankee pitched a perfect game during the season?

6. What Yankee finished third in the MVP voting?

7. Name the three Yankee pitchers who were not U.S. citizens
   who won ten or more games apiece during the regular season.

8. Name the four Yankees who hit more than 20 home runs
   during the season.

9. Only four Yankees have ever had back-to-back seasons of 120
   or more RBIs. What 1998 Yankee accomplished this?

10. For experts only: What was the only other franchise to win
    more regular season games in one season than the Yankees
    did in 1998?

ANSWERS

1. 114 + 3 + 4 + 4 = 125

2. Texas, Cleveland, and San Diego

3. Yankee Stadium and Shea Stadium — In April, a 100-pound joint fell from the Yankee Stadium roof, forcing the Yankees to play at Shea while it was being repaired.

4. Dwight Gooden of the Indians

5. David Wells

6. Derek Jeter

7. Hideki Irabu from Japan, Orlando Hernandez from Cuba and Ramiro Mendoza from Panama

8. Tino Martinez (28), Bernie Williams (26), Paul O'Neill (24) and Darryl Strawberry (24)

9. Tino Martinez — The other three were Babe Ruth, Lou Gehrig and Joe DiMaggio.

10. The 1906 Chicago Cubs finished 116-36.

Sec. 07

Row 19

Seat 12

Enter
Gate C
Upper Tier

"Catching a fly ball is a pleasure, but knowing what to do with it after you catch it is a business."

–Yankees outfielder Tommy Henrich

FULL SEASON TICKET

ICE CAPADES

1. What was the first NHL team based in New York?

2. The first coach of the Rangers had two sons and one grandson who also coached the Rangers. What's their family name?

3. Who was the first NY player to score 50 goals in a season?

4. How many Stanley Cups have the Rangers won?

5. How many Cups have the Islanders won?

6. How about the Devils?

7. Name one of the two former Ranger centers who coached the Islanders in their first year.

8. What New York player scored 50 or more goals for ten consecutive seasons?

9. Name the Islander goalie and the Devil goalie who have scored NHL goals.

10. For experts only: Who was the last man to be a player-coach of a New York NHL team?

Sec. 82   Row E   Seat 17   Enter Gate B

"Sorry, Mickey," the Lord said, "but I wanted to give you the word personally. You can't go to heaven because of the way you acted down on earth, but would you mind signing a dozen baseballs?"

–Mickey Mantle, *describing a recurring nightmare*

ANSWERS

1. The New York Americans — They started in 1925-'26, became the Brooklyn Americans in 1941-'42, and disbanded after that season. The Rangers began play in 1926.

2. Patrick — Lester was the first coach; his son Lynn coached in the '40s and son Muzz in the '50s; his grandson Craig took the reigns in the '80s.

3. Vic Hadfield, in 1971-'72

4. Four

5. Four

6. One

7. Phil Goyette and Earl Ingarfield

8. Mike Bossy

9. Billy Smith and Martin Brodeur

10. Doug Harvey of the Rangers, in the 1961-'62 season

FULL SEASON

Sec. 17
Row K
Seat 22
Gate F

"We didn't lose many games — and we never, never lost a party."

-Former Jet Curley Johnson, on his playing days with Joe Namath

THE JET SET

1. Before they were called the Jets, what was their nickname?

2. In what stadiums have the Jets played their home games?

3. The Jets won one AFL Championship Game. What team did they beat?

4. Who is the only Jet coach with a winning record?

5. What Jet set a record in 1984 with 22 sacks?

6. Name the four members of the Sack Exchange.

7. What Jet kicked 34 field goals in 1968, setting an NFL record that lasted 25 years?

8. Only once have the Jets had *the* number one pick in the NFL draft. Whom did they pick?

9. What Heisman-winning quarterback did they draft in 1965?

10. For experts only: The Jets have lost two AFC Championship Games. To what teams?

"I seldom refused autograph-seekers, unless they were old enough to look like collection agents."

-Joe Pepitone

Sec. 16

Row 51

Seat 7a

Enter Gate G
Lower Tier

ANSWERS

1. The Titans

2. Polo Grounds, Shea Stadium, and the Meadowlands (Giants Stadium)

3. Oakland Raiders

4. Bill Parcells

5. Mark Gastineau

6. Mark Gastineau, Joe Klecko, Marty Lyons and Abdul Salaam

7. Jim Turner

8. Keyshawn Johnson, in 1996

9. Johnny Huarte, of Notre Dame

10. Miami Dolphins and Denver Broncos

"I asked a guy what time it was, and he
said to me, 'What do I look like, a clock?'
That's when I knew I was home."

*–College basketball coach Jim Valvano,
on returning to New York*

Sec. 16

Row 51

Seat 7a

**Enter
Gate G**

Lower Tier

DEM BUMS

The Brooklyn Dodgers entered the National League in 1890 and moved to Los Angeles after the 1957 season. These questions refer to the Dodgers when they played in Brooklyn.

1. How many World Series did the Brooklyn Dodgers win?

2. In what year(s) did they win their World Series?

3. Name the manager(s) of their World Series-winning team(s).

4. Who played in every NY Yankee-Brooklyn Dodger World Series game?

5. Only one player has ever won the Cy Young Award, the Rookie of the Year Award and the MVP Award. Name this Dodger.

6. What Dodger first baseman won the first Rookie of the Year Award?

7. What three Brooklyn Dodgers hit more than 40 home runs in a season?

8. What Brooklyn Dodger pitcher won a World Series seventh game?

9. What member of the Dodgers pennant-winning teams in 1955 and '56 went on to pitch four no-hitters?

10. For experts only: The first baseman in the last game the Dodgers played in Brooklyn went on to hit 46 home runs for the Orioles in 1961. Can you name him?

ANSWERS

1. One

2. 1955

3. Walt Alston

4. Pee Wee Reese

5. Don Newcombe

6. Jackie Robinson — In 1948, he moved to second base.

7. Duke Snider, Roy Campanella and Gil Hodges

8. Johnny Podres

9. Sandy Koufax

10. Jim Gentile — Gil Hodges was the Dodgers starting third baseman that day.

FULL SEASON	Sec. 17 Row K Seat 22 Gate F	"On Father's Day, we again wish you all happy birthday."
		–Mets broadcaster and Hall of Famer Ralph Kiner

THE HIT PARADE

Each of the following describes a famous hit in New York sports history. See if you can identify it based on the hint given.

1. In one game, he homered against Hooton, Sosa and Hough.

2. His hit against Ulf Nilsson in 1979 earned him his own chant.

3. In 1951, he hit the "Shot Heard 'Round the World."

4. To Yankee fans, his ninth-inning '76 home run off Mark Littell was royal.

5. With two outs in the ninth inning, he broke up a World Series no-hitter.

6. George Brett's home run against what Yankee pitcher created the Pine Tar Game?

7. Chuck Bednarik's giant hit against what NY player caused the player to take a one-year sabbatical?

8. His grounder to Bill Buckner in Game Six turned Buckner into a goat.

9. His 61st was against Tracy Stallard.

10. For experts only: Name the two Yankees who homered in the Yankees 163rd regular-season game of 1978.

ANSWERS

1. Reggie Jackson hit three home runs off three different Dodger pitchers in the last game of the 1977 World Series.

2. Denis Potvin of the Islanders — He has been retired over ten seasons and some Ranger fans *still* chant his name at games.

3. Bobby Thomson

4. Chris Chambliss — His home run ended the game and put the Yankees in the Series for the first time in twelve years.

5. Cookie Lavagetto of the Brooklyn Dodgers, in 1947 — His double off Bill Bevans was the Dodgers first hit and won the game, 3-2.

6. Goose Gossage

7. Frank Gifford

8. Mookie Wilson

9. Roger Maris

10. Bucky Dent and Reggie Jackson — This was the Yankee-Red Sox playoff game which determined the American League East champion.

1969
THE MIRACLE METS

Although the Mets had never finished better than ninth before this year, they shocked the baseball world by winning it all in 1969. Test your knowledge of that incredible season.

1. What team finished second in the NL East that year?

2. What NL team did the Mets beat in the playoffs?

3. Name the brothers who were teammates on the Mets playoff opponents.

4. There were three eventual 300-game winners who pitched in the NL division playoff. How many do you know?

5. What Met and what Oriole who appeared in the World Series eventually became Met managers?

6. On September 15, Steve Carlton struck out 19 Mets. Who hit two two-run home runs off him to give the Mets a 4-3 victory?

7. Two Met regulars finished with .300 batting averages that year. Do you know either one?

8. What three Met pitchers won in double figures during the regular season. (Hint: Each won a World Series game that year.)

9. What Met had won an AL Rookie of the Year Award while playing for the White Sox?

10 For experts only: Name three of the four Mets who hit home runs in the '69 World Series.

ANSWERS

1. Chicago Cubs
2. Atlanta Braves
3. Hank and Tommie Aaron
4. Tom Seaver, Nolan Ryan and Phil Niekro
5. Davey Johnson and Bud Harrelson
6. Ron Swoboda
7. Cleon Jones (.340) and Art Shamsky (.300)
8. Tom Seaver (23), Jerry Koosman (17) and Gary Gentry (13)
9. Tommie Agee
10. Tommie Agee, Donn Clendenon, Ed Kranepool and Al Weis

FULL SEASON

| Sec. 17 | Row K | Seat 22 | Gate F |

"We've got a problem here. Luis Tiant wants to use the bathroom, and it says no foreign objects in the toilet."

-Yankees third baseman Craig Nettles, on a plane with the Cuban pitcher

NAMES AND NUMBERS

Each of the following one-digit numerals has been retired by the team listed. Name the players.

1. Dodgers - #1
2. Yankees - #1
3. Rangers - #1
4. Yankees - #4
5. Dodgers - #4
6. Baseball Giants - #4
7. Islanders - #5
8. Yankees - #7
9. Rangers - #7
10. Yankees - #9

"Rooting for the Yankees is like rooting for U.S. Steel."

–Sports columnist Red Smith

Sec. 16

Row 51

Seat 7a

**Enter
Gate G**
Lower Tier

ANSWERS

1. Pee Wee Reese
2. Billy Martin
3. Ed Giacomin
4. Lou Gehrig
5. Duke Snider
6. Mel Ott
7. Denis Potvin
8. Mickey Mantle
9. Rod Gilbert
10. Roger Maris

Sec. 07

Row 19

Seat 12

Enter
Gate C
Upper Tier

"**When you get old, everything is hurting. When I get up in the morning, it sounds like I'm making popcorn.**"

–Giants linebacker Lawrence Taylor, on turning 33

FULL SEASON TICKET

NO-HITTERS

1. Name all the pitchers who have thrown no-hitters as Mets.

2. The 1969 Mets had three pitchers who threw no-hitters during their careers (but not as Mets). Name two of them.

3. Who pitched the only World Series no-hitter?

4. What Yankee threw a Fourth of July no-hitter?

5. What knuckleballing Oriole (and former Giant who pitched until he was 49) threw a no-hitter against the Yanks in 1958?

6. What Yankee pitched two no-hitters in the 1951 season?

7. What United States Senator threw a perfect game against the Mets in 1964?

8. What Davids were Goliath in terms of perfect games for the Yankees in 1998 and '99?

9. What former Met has the record for most career no-hitters?

10. For experts only: Name the last batter in the only World Series perfect game.

Sec. Row Seat
82 E 17

Enter Gate B

"Phil Jackson is one of the most intelligent players I ever saw. He's so smart he can commit 12 fouls and only get caught for 4."

–Knicks coach Red Holtzman

ANSWERS

1. No Met has ever thrown a no-hitter (as a Met).

2. Don Cardwell, Nolan Ryan and Tom Seaver

3. Don Larsen, in 1956

4. Dave Righetti, in 1983

5. Hoyt Wilhelm

6. Allie Reynolds

7. Jim Bunning of the Phillies

8. David Wells and David Cone

9. Nolan Ryan threw *seven*.

10. Dale Mitchell of the Dodgers

"There were the inevitable comparisons
from day one. But they ended on day two."

*-Power Memorial High School center
Len Elmore, on replacing Lew Alcindor
(Kareem Abdul-Jabbar)*

| Sec. 16 |
| Row 51 |
| Seat 7a |

**Enter
Gate G**
Lower Tier

THE NAME GAME

Do you know the real first names of the first five players listed below and the nicknames of the last five?

1. Yogi Berra
2. Mickey Mantle
3. Tino Martinez
4. Cazzie Russell
5. Mookie Wilson
6. Roger Clemens
7. Julius Erving
8. Walt Frazier
9. Wayne Gretzky
10. Bill Parcells

Sec. 82 Row E Seat 17 Enter Gate B

"Alright everyone, line up alphabetically according to your height."

-Yankees manager Casey Stengel

ANSWERS

1. Lawrence

2. Mickey

3. Constantino

4. Cazzie

5. William

6. The Rocket

7. Dr. J

8. Clyde

9. The Great Gretzky or The Great One

10. Tuna — Ironically, "Bill" is also a nickname; his given name is Duane Charles Parcells.

Sec. 07

Row 19

Seat 12

Enter
Gate C

Upper Tier

**"The only sure rule in golf is —
he who has the fastest cart never
has to play bad lie."**

–Mickey Mantle

FULL SEASON TICKET

QUEENS QUICKIES

Answer the following questions which refer to the New York City borough of Queens.

1. What jockey won six Belmont Stakes in Queens?

2. What horse won the Belmont by 31 lengths in 1973?

3. In what decade was the last NFL football game played in Queens?

4. True or false? Golf's U.S. Open has been held in Queens.

5. The United States Tennis Championships are also held in Queens. What one-time resident of Queens won four U.S. Men's Singles Championships?

6. What woman, upon winning the Open in Queens, completed a sweep of the four Grand Slam tennis tournaments in 1988?

7. True or false? The Yankees have played more than 100 regular-season games in Queens.

8. What Queens college has made it to the NCAA Division I Basketball Championship Game?

9. Who has hit the most major league home runs in Queens?

10. For experts only: The Mets played in the World Series in 1969, '73 and '86. How many World Series games did they win in Queens?

ANSWERS

1. Eddie Arcaro

2. Secretariat

3. The 1980s — The Jets last year at Shea was 1983.

4. True, in 1932 at the Fresh Meadows C.C. in Flushing

5. John McEnroe

6. Steffi Graf

7. True — They played their home games at Shea in 1974 and '75.

8. St. Johns — They lost to Kansas in 1952.

9. Darryl Strawberry

10. Seven — three in '69, two each in '73 and '86

"David Cone is in a class by himself with three or four other players."

–*Yankees owner George Steinbrenner*

| Sec. 16 |
| Row 51 |
| Seat 7a |
| Enter Gate G |
| Lower Tier |

NETS NOTES

1. How many ABA Championships did the Nets win?

2. What Net was ABA MVP for three consecutive years?

3. What player who wound up being a six-time NBA MVP was the Nets number one draft pick in 1969?

4. In their first year of existence, the team wasn't called the Nets. What was the team nickname?

5. True or false? The Nets were called the New York Nets for four seasons.

6. The Nets are one of the four ABA teams who entered the NBA. Do you know the other three?

7. Since joining the NBA, only once have the Nets had *the* number one pick in the draft. What Syracuse player did they pick in 1990?

8. What St. John's coach coached the Nets?

9. In the 1996 and '97 drafts, the Nets picked Villanova players in the first round. Name them.

10. For experts only: Three Nets were ABA First Team All-Stars. How many can you get?

ANSWERS

1. Two, 1973-'74 and 1975-'76

2. Julius Erving in 1973-'74, 1974-'75 and 1975-'76

3. Lew Alcindor (who later changed his name to Kareem Abdul-Jabbar) — He was also drafted number one by the NBA Milwaukee Bucks and signed with them.

4. New Jersey Americans

5. True, from the 1968-'69 season through 1971-'72

6. Denver Nuggets, Indiana Pacers and San Antonio Spurs

7. Derrick Coleman

8. Lou Carnesecca

9. Kerry Kittles and Tim Thomas

10. Rick Barry (1971 and '72), Bill Melchionni (1972) and Julius Erving (1974, '75 and '76)

> "I really love playing and living in New York. There's such a high energy here. Everybody's fighting for the same cab."
>
> *–Hockey great Wayne Gretzky*

Sec. 82   Row E   Seat 17   Enter Gate B

PRIZE PACKAGES

Below are clues to players who have won MVP Awards.
Name at least one player for each description.

1. A Knick

2. A Jet in the Super Bowl

3. A Giant in the Super Bowl

4. A Ranger (since 1960)

5. An Islander

6. A Yankee shortstop (in 1950)

7. A Met

8. A baseball New York Giant (since 1950)

9. A player who started with the Mets, but won while with a different team

10. For experts only: A player who started with the Yankees, but, in 1958, won while with the Red Sox

---

FULL SEASON

Sec. 17
Row K
Seat 22
Gate F

"You gotta be a man to play baseball for a living but you gotta have a lot of little boy in you, too."

–Brooklyn Dodgers catcher Roy Campanella

ANSWERS

1. Willis Reed

2. Joe Namath

3. Phil Simms and Ottis Anderson

4. Mark Messier

5. Bryan Trottier, in 1979

6. Phil Rizzuto

7. I hope that you didn't rack your brains on this one — No Met has ever been selected MVP.

8. Willie Mays, in 1954

9. Kevin Mitchell, in 1989 while with the Reds

10. Jackie Jensen

FULL SEASON

Sec. 17
Row K
Seat 22
Gate F

"The Bulls had me in for a four-hour psychological test, and the next day they went out and signed Dennis Rodman."

–Nets center Jayson Williams, in 1995

BACKSTOP BRAINBUSTERS

1. Name the two catchers who won three MVP Awards apiece.

2. What Met holds the major league record for most home runs by a catcher in a season?

3. The 1961 Yankee team had three players who caught games that year and hit more than 20 home runs apiece. Name them.

4. The Yankees retired number 8 for two catchers. Who?

5. The player with the most career pinch-hit home runs played for the Yankees in 1977 and '78. Name this catcher and designated hitter whose initials are C.J.

6. What Met catcher had 25 stolen bases in a season?

7. What catcher had nine hits and batted .529 in the 1976 World Series?

8. Name two of the three Yankee catchers who became Yankee managers.

9. What Met catcher holds the club's consecutive game hitting streak record?

10. For experts only: The Mets number one pick in the 1962 expansion draft was a catcher from the San Francisco Giants. Who is he?

ANSWERS

1. Yogi Berra and Roy Campanella

2. Todd Hundley

3. Yogi Berra, John Blanchard and Elston Howard —
   Note: They did not hit all of these home runs as catchers.

4. Yogi Berra and Bill Dickey

5. Cliff Johnson

6. John Stearns

7. Thurman Munson — He went 9 for 17 against the Reds.
   Johnny Bench of the Reds was the World Series MVP but
   had "only" eight hits while batting .533.

8. Yogi Berra, Bill Dickey and Ralph Houk

9. Mike Piazza, 24 games — He shares this record with Hubie
   Brooks.

10. Hobie Landrith — When asked why he picked a catcher first,
    Casey Stengel said that without one you get a lot of
    passed balls.

Sec. 07

Row 19

Seat 12

Enter
Gate C
Upper Tier

FULL SEASON TICKET

**"They pay me to practice during the week.
On Sunday I play for nothing."**

–Jets linebacker Greg Buttle

THE ICING
ON THE CAKE

The Rangers won the Stanley Cup in 1994 for the first time in over fifty years. How well do you remember that team?

1. Name the Rangers head coach and their general manager.

2. What four teams did they beat in the playoffs?

3. Who was the Rangers leading scorer in the regular season? (Hint: He was a defenseman.)

4. Who scored two double-overtime goals in the playoffs for the Rangers that year?

5. Name the two Rangers goalies.

6. Who was the MVP of the playoffs?

7. Who scored the winning goal in the Stanley Cup-clinching game?

8. What was the previous year in which the Rangers had won the Cup?

9. Can you come up with the four Russians on the '94 team?

10. For experts only: Name four of the six players on ice when the Rangers won the Cup.

ANSWERS

1. Coach — Mike Keenan and General Manager — Neil Smith

2. The Islanders, Washington Capitals, New Jersey Devils and Vancouver Canucks

3. Sergei Zubov

4. Stephane Matteau

5. Mike Richter and Glen Healy

6. Brian Leetch

7. Mark Messier

8. 1940

9. Alexander Karpovtsev, Alexei Kovalev, Sergei Nemchinov and Sergei Zubov

10. Steve Larmer, Brian Leetch, Doug Lidster, Craig MacTavish, Mark Messier and Mike Richter

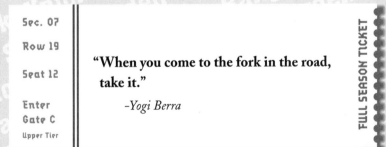

Sec. 07

Row 19

Seat 12

Enter
Gate C
Upper Tier

"When you come to the fork in the road, take it."

–Yogi Berra

FULL SEASON TICKET

RUTH AND GEHRIG

1. What were their full names?

2. What number did Babe Ruth wear when he first came to the Yanks?

3. Name their retired numbers.

4. How many regular-season home runs did Ruth hit?

5. How many times did each hit 50 or more home runs in a season?

6. Is it fact or fiction that Ruth once hit more home runs in a season than all the other teams in the American League combined?

7. What New York college did Lou Gehrig attend?

8. How many consecutive games did Gehrig play?

9. What were the titles of the movies made about Ruth and Gehrig? Name the actors who portrayed them.

10. For experts only: Lou Gehrig holds the record for career grand slams. How many?

ANSWERS

1. George Herman Ruth and Henry Louis Gehrig

2. No number — The Yankees didn't have numbers on their uniforms until the 1929 season.

3. Ruth, 3 and Gehrig, 4 — They were assigned these numbers because of their usual places in the batting order.

4. 714

5. Gehrig, none — The most he hit was 49, which he did twice; Ruth, four times.

6. Fiction

7. Columbia University

8. 2,130

9. *The Babe Ruth Story* — The Babe was played by William Bendix and *The Pride of the Yankees* — Gary Cooper played Gehrig (and Babe Ruth played himself).

10. 23

"Every time I look at my pocketbook, I see Jackie Robinson."

-New York Giants outfielder Willie Mays

| Sec. 16 |
| Row 51 |
| Seat 7a |
| Enter Gate G Lower Tier |

STADIA-MANIA

Identify the New York venues described below.

1. It's where the Islanders play.

2. It used to be Brendan Byrne Arena.

3. Beatles, Cubs, and Dolphins have played there.

4. It was built on Coogan's Bluff.

5. It's where they hold the finals of the United States Tennis Championships.

6. Its monuments used to be on the field of play.

7. Army plays most of its home football games here.

8. The first Ali-Frazier fight was held here.

9. The Dodgers played here from 1913 to 1957.

10. For experts only: Name one of the two existing Manhattan stadiums north of the Empire State Building.

Sec. 82   Row E   Seat 17   Enter Gate B

"You know, if you kill somebody, they sentence you to life, you serve twenty years, and you get paroled. I never got paroled."

–Brooklyn Dodgers pitcher Ralph Branca, never forgiven for serving up the "shot heard 'round the world," Bobby Thomson's 1951 pennant-winning homer for the New York Giants

ANSWERS

1. Nassau Veterans Memorial Coliseum

2. Continental Airlines Arena

3. Shea Stadium

4. The Polo Grounds

5. Arthur Ashe Stadium

6. Yankee Stadium — The monuments used to be located in center field, in front of the fence 461 feet from home plate. After the renovation in the 1970s, the outfield fence was moved in, and Monument Park was built behind the center field wall.

7. Michie Stadium

8. Madison Square Garden

9. Ebbets Field

10. Downing Stadium (on Randalls Island), where the Cosmos played, and Wein Stadium at Baker Field, the athletic field of Columbia University

---

Sec. 07

Row 19

Seat 12

Enter
Gate C

Upper Tier

FULL SEASON TICKET

"When we lost, I couldn't sleep at night. When we win, I can't sleep at night. But when you win, you wake up feeling better."

–Yankees manager Joe Torre

MET MILESTONES

Which players accomplished the following as Mets?

1. Set the Met record of 227 hits in a season (in 1996)

2. Batman who hit a grand slam in each game of a doubleheader (in 1999)

3. Met career leader in steals and triples

4. Won and lost 20 games in different seasons

5. Future Yankee finished with a 20-3 record in 1988

6. Won the league RBI title

7. Had the best Met batting average in a season — .353, in 1998

8. Won 25 games in a season

9. Won the pitcher's Triple Crown in 1985, leading the league in wins, strikeouts and ERA

10. For experts only: Met pitcher with most career losses

"If my quarterback runs, I'll shoot him."

–Jets coach Bill Parcells, on his version of the "run and shoot" offense

Sec. 16

Row 51

Seat 7a

**Enter
Gate G**
Lower Tier

ANSWERS

1. Lance Johnson
2. Robin Ventura — No other player in the majors has ever done this.
3. Mookie Wilson
4. Jerry Koosman — In 1976, he won 21; in '77, he lost 20.
5. David Cone
6. Howard Johnson, in 1991
7. John Olerud
8. Tom Seaver, in 1969
9. Dwight Gooden
10. Jerry Koosman (137)

FULL SEASON

Sec. 17
Row K
Seat 22
Gate F

"The only reason I don't like playing in the World Series is I can't watch myself play."

–Mr. October, Reggie Jackson

PIGSKIN POTPOURRI

1. The Giants 1952 number one pick from USC holds the team record for career touchdowns. Who is he?

2. Who was the Giants general manager when they won their Super Bowls?

3. The Giants number one pick in 1969 went on to star in the TV program *Hunter* in the '80s. Name him.

4. Until Dan Marino broke the record in 1984, what Giant quarterback had thrown the most touchdown passes in a season?

5. From 1954 through '58, the Giants had two assistant coaches who later went on to be head coaches of Super Bowl-winning teams. Who are they?

6. The Jets played in the first *Monday Night Football* game (in 1970). Against what team? Did they win or lose?

7. What Jet is the only NFL defensive player to make the Pro Bowl at three different positions? (Hint: He was also in the movies *Smokey and the Bandit II* and *Cannonball Run.*)

8. Who is the Jets career rushing leader?

9. Three picks before the Dolphins selected Dan Marino in the 1983 NFL draft, the Jets chose a quarterback. Who?

10. For experts only: What Jet was the AFC's leading receiver in the '87 and '88 seasons?

ANSWERS

1. Frank Gifford
2. George Young
3. Fred Dryer
4. Y.A. Tittle
5. Tom Landry and Vince Lombardi
6. Cleveland beat them, 31-21.
7. Joe Klecko
8. Freeman McNeil
9. Ken O'Brien
10. Al Toon

Sec. 07

Row 19

Seat 12

Enter
Gate C

Upper Tier

"Being with a woman all night never hurt no professional baseball player. It's staying up all night looking for a woman that does him in."

–Yankees manager Casey Stengel

FULL SEASON TICKET

KNIGHTLY KNICKS

1. How many championships have the Knicks won?

2. Name the coach of these teams.

3. What team(s) did they beat in the Finals?

4. Name the playoff MVPs in these years.

5. What member of these teams became a U.S. Senator?

6. Name a player on these teams who became ABA commissioner.

7. What Knick on these teams was the club's "territorial choice" in 1965?

8. What championship Knick pitched for the White Sox?

9. What future Knick head coach played on these teams?

10. For experts only: What member of one of these teams had a son who was the second pick in the 1998 NBA draft and also had a brother who pitched a no-hitter in the majors?

Sec. 82   Row E   Seat 17   Enter Gate B

"When they operated, I told them to put in a Koufax fastball. They did — but it was a Mrs. Koufax fastball."

–Yankees pitcher Tommy John, on his reconstructive arm surgery

ANSWERS

1. Two

2. Red Holzman

3. The Los Angeles Lakers, both times

4. Willis Reed, again both times

5. Bill Bradley

6. Dave DeBusschere

7. Bill Bradley

8. Dave DeBusschere

9. Willis Reed

10. Henry Bibby — His son Mike was picked by Vancouver; his brother Jim threw a no-hitter for Texas in 1973.

"When I was a little boy, I wanted to be a baseball player and join the circus. With the Yankees I've accomplished both."

*-Yankees third baseman Graig Nettles, on
the turbulent George Steinbrenner years*

| Sec. 16 |
| Row 51 |
| Seat 7a |

**Enter
Gate G**
Lower Tier

BATTLE OF BUCKNER HILL

The Mets capped off a dominating season in 1986 with a seven-game victory over the Red Sox. Here are some baseball bafflers on the Bill Buckner-bashing Series.

1. Within five, how many regular season games did the Mets win?

2. Six pitchers won 10 or more games during the regular season. How many do you know?

3. What player who had hit 52 home runs during the 1977 season played for the Mets in 1986?

4. Two players who went on to win home run titles (one with the Mets, one for another team) played shortstop for the Mets that year. Who are they?

5. What NL West team was the Mets opponent in the playoffs?

6. Who had a pinch-hit from both sides of the plate in the World Series?

7. What three Mets got hits in the tenth inning of game 6 of the World Series?

8. Who was the World Series MVP?

9. What '86 Met went on to pitch more games in the majors then any other pitcher in history?

10. For experts only: What former Met lost games 6 and 7 of the World Series?

ANSWERS

1. 108 — They finished 108-54.

2. Dwight Gooden (17), Ron Darling (15), Bob Ojeda (18), Sid Fernandez (16), Rick Aguilera (10) Roger McDowell (14)

3. George Foster — He was released in August.

4. Howard Johnson and Kevin Mitchell

5. Houston Astros

6. Lee Mazzilli

7. Gary Carter, Kevin Mitchell and Ray Knight

8. Ray Knight

9. Jesse Orosco

10. Calvin Schiraldi

FULL SEASON

Sec. 17
Row K
Seat 22
Gate F

"Sevy's been playing quietly very well of late, and he had that Gordie Howe hat trick- a goal, an assist and a fight."

-Islanders coach Mike Milbury, on defenseman Brent Severyn

FORE!

1. What Westchester County golf course has been the site of four U.S. Opens?

2. Do you know the Suffolk County golf course which hosted the second U.S. Open in 1896 and another one 99 years later?

3. What Bronx golf course is the oldest municipal course in the United States and the one at which Kramer from *Seinfeld* plays?

4. What Rochester, NY golf club has hosted three U.S. Opens?

5. What golfer successfully defended his U.S. Open championship at this Rochester course in 1989?

6. The first PGA Championship was held at the Siwanoy Country Club in 1916. In what NY county is Siwanoy?

7. Since 1940, the PGA Championship has been held in New York State twice. Can you name either course?

8. Four men have won all four Grand Slam championships during their careers. Name the New Yorker who accomplished this.

9. The U.S. Open will be held at what public golf course in New York in 2002?

10. For experts only: The oldest continuous golf club in the United States is located in New York. Name it. (Hint: It's the namesake of a famous British course.)

ANSWERS

1. Winged Foot, in Mamaroneck
2. Shinnecock Hills
3. Van Cortlandt Golf Course
4. Oak Hill
5. Curtis Strange — Ironically, that was his last PGA win on tour.
6. Westchester — It is located in Bronxville.
7. Oak Hill, in 1980 and Winged Foot, in 1997
8. Gene Sarazen of Harrison
9. The Black Course at Bethpage State Park, on Long Island
10. St. Andrews, which used to be in Yonkers and is now in Hastings

FULL SEASON

Sec. 17 Row K Seat 22 Gate F

"I had only one superstition. I made sure to touch all the bases when I hit a home run."

–Babe Ruth

BROACHING COACHING

Identify the man from the clue.

1. Managed and played for both the Mets and Yankees

2. Coached both Jets and Giants

3. Managed both Dodgers and Giants

4. Managed ten Yankee pennant winners

5. Coached the Knicks the last time they lost in the Finals

6. Was the first African-American head coach of a major professional team in NYC

7. Coached the Super Bowl Giants

8. Coached the Rangers, the Devils and the U.S. Olympic hockey team

9. Coached both the Jets and Notre Dame

10. For experts only: Name the man who pitched four games for the Mets and later managed the Mets and Yankees.

Sec. 07

Row 19

Seat 12

Enter
Gate C
Upper Tier

"When I get through managing, I'm going to open up a kindergarten."

–Billy Martin

FULL SEASON TICKET

ANSWERS

1. Yogi Berra
2. Bill Parcells
3. Leo Durocher
4. Casey Stengel
5. Jeff Van Gundy
6. Willis Reed
7. Bill Parcells
8. Herb Brooks
9. Lou Holtz
10. Dallas Green

Sec.	Row	Seat	Enter Gate B
82	E	17	

"The similarities between me and my father are different."

–Former big leaguer Dale Berra, the son of that master of malaprops, Yogi Berra

1961 YANKEES

The 1961 Yankee team was one of the best of all time. Test your "Sports Wiz" abilities with a quiz about that team.

1. What pitcher won 25 games for them that year?

2. How many home runs did Mickey Mantle and Roger Maris combine for that year?

3. Who was the league MVP (for the second year in a row)?

4. Name their new manager.

5. How many intentional walks did Maris get that year?

6. Within five, how many regular season games did they win?

7. What team did they defeat in the World Series?

8. In that year's Series, a pitcher broke a record (which he started in a previous Series) with 32 consecutive scoreless innings. Name this pitcher.

9. Whose World Series record of 29 2/3 consecutive scoreless innings did he break?

10. For experts only: Name the usual eight position players for the Yankees that year.

ANSWERS

1. Whitey Ford

2. 115 (61 for Maris and 54 for Mantle)

3. Roger Maris

4. Ralph Houk

5. None — Obviously, Mickey Mantle batting behind him had something to do with that. A year later, with Mantle out of the line-up, Maris was walked intentionally four times in *one* game.

6. 109 — They were 109-53.

7. Cincinnati

8. Whitey Ford

9. Babe Ruth, when he was with the Red Sox

10. 1B — Bill Skowron, 2B — Bobby Richardson, SS — Tony Kubek, 3B — Clete Boyer, LF — Yogi Berra, CF — Mickey Mantle, RF — Roger Maris and C — Elston Howard

Sec. 82   Row E   Seat 17   Enter Gate B

"I could never play in New York. The first time I ever came into a game there, I got in the bullpen car and they told me to lock the door."

–*Baltimore Orioles pitcher Mike Flanagan*

THE KNICKS - GIVE ME A DRAFT

Match the following number-one picks of the Knicks with the colleges they attended.

1.	Greg Anthony	a)	DePaul
2.	Bill Bradley	b)	Florida State
3.	Bill Cartwright	c)	Georgetown
4.	Hubert Davis	d)	Michigan
5.	Patrick Ewing	e)	North Carolina
6.	Walt Frazier	f)	Princeton
7.	Mark Jackson	g)	St. Johns
8.	Cazzie Russell	h)	San Francisco
9.	Rod Strickland	i)	Southern Illinois
10.	Charlie Ward	j)	UNLV

Sec. 07

Row 19

Seat 12

Enter
Gate C
Upper Tier

**"I was driving on the highway in New Jersey and saw a sign.
It said, 'Interstate 95, Nets 91.'"**

–Basketballer turned broadcaster John Salley

FULL SEASON TICKET

ANSWERS

1. J
2. F
3. H
4. E
5. C
6. I
7. G
8. D
9. A
10. B

"Baseball is like church. Many attend, but few understand."

–Mets manager Wes Westrum

| Sec. 16 |
| Row 51 |
| Seat 7a |
| Enter Gate G Lower Tier |

SCHOOL DAYS

Match the New York colleges on the left with the NCAA
Division I Men's Championships or NIT Championships
which they won on the right.

1. Army

2. CCNY

3. Columbia

4. Cornell

5. LIU

6. Manhattan

7. Renssalaer

8. St. Bonaventures

9. St. Johns

10. Syracuse

a) Fencing — 11 times

b) Football — 1914, '44, '45

c) Hockey — 1954, '85

d) Hockey — 1967; lacrosse — 1971, '76, '77
   football — 1915, '21, '22

e) Indoor track and field — 1973

f) Lacrosse — 1983, '88, '89, '90, '93, '95

g) NCAA and NIT basketball — 1950

h) NIT basketball — 1939, '41

i) NIT basketball — 1977

j) Soccer — 1996
   NIT basketball — 1943, '44, '59, '65, '89

Sec. 82   Row E   Seat 17   Enter Gate B

"That may have been the best game you
ever pitched."

*-Yogi Berra, talking to Don Larsen who had
just hurled the only perfect game in World
Series history*

ANSWERS

1. B
2. G
3. A
4. D
5. H
6. E
7. C
8. I
9. J
10. F

FULL SEASON

Sec. 17
Row K
Seat 22
Gate F

"Ain't no sense in worrying about things you got control over, 'cause if you got control over them, ain't no sense worrying. And there ain't no sense worrying about things you got no control over, 'cause if you got no control over them, ain't no sense worrying about them."

–Yankees outfielder Mickey Rivers

MAPPING IT OUT

1. Where in New York State have the Olympics been held?

2. The football Giants have played their home games in three states. Can you name them?

3. In what town is the Baseball Hall of Fame located?

4. The Knicks played the first game in NBA history. They played on the road against the Huskies. In what foreign city did they play?

5. In the 1950s, the Dodgers played some home games in what New Jersey city?

6. In 1999, the Yankees opened a minor league team in what NYC borough?

7. Name the three upstate NY cities which used to have NBA teams.

8. Who fought 17 heavyweight championship fights in NYC?

9. The New York Marathon begins in what borough?

10. For experts only: List (in order) the boroughs through which you run the entire marathon.

ANSWERS

1. Lake Placid - 1932 and '80

2. New York, Connecticut (at the Yale Bowl while Yankee Stadium was being renovated) and New Jersey

3. Cooperstown, New York

4. Toronto

5. Jersey City

6. Staten Island

7. Rochester Royals, Syracuse Nationals and Buffalo Braves

8. Joe Louis

9. Staten Island

10. Staten Island, Brooklyn, Queens, Manhattan, the Bronx and Manhattan again

Sec. 07

Row 19

Seat 12

Enter
Gate C
Upper Tier

"**If hockey fights were fixed, you'd see me in more of them.**"

–Former Ranger Rod Gilbert

FULL SEASON TICKET

ANAGRAMS

Below are anagrams of the last names of Mets and Yankees
who have led their teams (not necessarily their leagues) in
home runs. To make it a little easier, the years in which each
led have been listed. How many can you decode? (Hint: The
first five are Mets; the last five, Yankees.)

1. A PIZZA - 1998

2. NO BRAG - 1995

3. CRATER - 1985

4. A NO BILL - 1992-'94

5. O BLOODY GUN - 1979

6. I AM SWILL - 1996

7. LIL' ONE - 1994-'95

8. LET MAN - 1954-'60, '64, '67, '68

9. HER GIG - 1931, '34-'36

10. PIPE NOTE - 1966, '69

FULL SEASON	Sec. 17 Row K Seat 22 Gate F	"Basketball can serve as a kind of metaphor for ultimate cooperation. It is a sport where success, as symbolized by the championship, requires that the dictates of community prevail over selfish personal impulses."

–New York Knicks forward Bill Bradley

ANSWERS

1. Mike PIAZZA
2. Rico BROGNA
3. Gary CARTER
4. Bobby BONILLA
5. Joel YOUNGBLOOD
6. Bernie WILLIAMS
7. Paul O'NEILL
8. Mickey MANTLE
9. Lou GEHRIG
10. Joe PEPITONE

"We're experiencing audio difficulties."

–Mets broadcaster Ralph Kiner,
while on the air

| Sec. 16 |
| Row 51 |
| Seat 7a |
| Enter
Gate G
Lower Tier |

HORSING AROUND

Here are some nagging questions about the Belmont.

1. In which borough is the Belmont Stakes currently held?

2. *My Old Kentucky Home* is played before the start of the Kentucky Derby. What song is played before the beginning of the Belmont Stakes?

3. In what other New York borough was this race previously held?

4. Which of the other two Triple Crown races has also been held in New York?

5. What is the current distance of the Belmont?

6. What horse holds the record time for this race at the current distance?

7. Only once have there been back-to-back Triple Crown winners. What horses achieved this in 1977 and '78?

8. The only female jockey to win a Triple Crown race did so in New York. Who is she?

9. True or false? Two Triple Crown races were once held on the same day at the same track.

10. For experts only: In 1997 through '99, horses won the first two legs of the Triple Crown but were upset at the Belmont. Name the three horses that lost and the three winners of the Belmont Stakes during those years.

ANSWERS

1. Queens

2. *Sidewalks of New York* (East Side, West Side)

3. The Bronx — From 1867-'89, it was held at Jerome Park and from 1890-1904, at Morris Park.

4. The Preakness — It was held in 1890 at Morris Park in the Bronx and, from 1894-1908, at Gravesend Park in Brooklyn. In 1909, it moved back to Pimlico (where it had started in 1873).

5. One-and-a-half miles

6. Secretariat (2:24)

7. Seattle Slew, in 1977 and Affirmed, in 1978

8. Julie Krone — She won the 1993 Belmont aboard Colonial Affair.

9. True — In 1890, both were run at Morris Park in the Bronx. The Preakness was the second race and the Belmont the fourth that day.

10. In 1997, Silver Charm won the first two races but lost to Touch Gold at the Belmont; in 1998, Victory Gallop nosed out Real Quiet to prevent him from sweeping the Triple Crown; in 1999, Lemon Drop Kid won at Belmont after Charismatic had won the Derby and the Preakness.

NAMES AND NUMBERS II

Each of the following two-digit numerals has been retired by the team listed. Name the players.

1. Yankees - #10
2. Knicks - #10
3. Jets - #12
4. Mets - #14
5. Football Giants - #11
6. Knicks - #15
7. Knicks - #19
8. Nets - #23
9. Yanks and Mets - #37
10. Football Giants - #56

Sec. 82 | Row E | Seat 17

Enter Gate B

"It's just ice. That doesn't mean they're hurt."

–Bill Parcells, then the coach of the Giants, explaining the bags players wear on their knees and elbows after a football game

ANSWERS

1. Phil Rizzuto
2. Walt Frazier
3. Joe Namath
4. Gil Hodges
5. Phil Simms
6. Earl Monroe and Dick McGuire
7. Willis Reed
8. John Williamson
9. Casey Stengel
10. Lawrence Taylor

"If the people don't want to come out to the park, nobody's going to stop 'em."

–Yogi Berra

Sec. 16

Row 51

Seat 7a

Enter Gate G
Lower Tier

FOUR-PEAT'S SAKE

During the 1980s, the Islanders won four consecutive Stanley Cups. See how much you know about those Islander teams.

1. Name the Islanders head coach and their general manager.

2. Name the Islander goalies who won playoff victories during those years.

3. Who scored the Isles first Stanley Cup-winning goal?

4. Four different players won playoff MVP Awards during those years. Name them.

5. Who scored a record seven goals in the 1982 final four-game sweep?

6. What were the four teams that the Isles defeated in the finals?

7. What team ended the dynasty?

8. What Islander scored four playoff overtime goals?

9. What three-time winner of the Norris Trophy as best defenseman was on these teams?

10. For experts only: The Islanders won their first Stanley Cup with an overtime goal. You're lucky if you can give the time of this goal.

ANSWERS

1. Coach — Al Arbour and General Manager — Bill Torrey

2. Billy Smith and Rollie Melanson

3. Bob Nystrom

4. Bryan Trottier (1980), Butch Goring (1981), Mike Bossy (1982) and Billy Smith (1983)

5. Mike Bossy

6. Philadelphia Flyers, Minnesota North Stars, Vancouver Canucks and Edmonton Oilers

7. Edmonton Oilers, in 1983

8. Bob Nystrom

9. Denis Potvin

10. 7:11 of the first overtime period

Sec. **82** Row **E** Seat **17**

Enter Gate B

"We needed to buy a vowel."

–Mets general manager Steve Phillips, explaining the signing of infielder Robert Eenhoorn

JETS ON HIGH

The Jets surprised everyone when they won the Super Bowl in January, 1969 despite being 18-point underdogs. The following questions refer to that Jets team.

1. What number Super Bowl did the Jets win?

2. Who was their head coach?

3. What team did they beat?

4. Who was their coach?

5. What was the score of the game?

6. What Jet scored a touchdown?

7. Who was MVP of the game?

8. Where was the game played?

9. What Jet was the leading scorer in the game and the season?

10. For experts only: Name the four quarterbacks who played during the game.

| FULL SEASON | Sec. 17 Row K Seat 22 Gate F | **"When you win, nothing hurts."** *–Joe Namath* |

ANSWERS

1. Super Bowl III

2. Weeb Ewbank

3. Baltimore Colts

4. Don Shula

5. 16-7

6. Matt Snell

7. Joe Namath

8. The Orange Bowl in Miami

9. Jim Turner — He kicked three field goals and a point-after-touchdown in the game.

10. Jets — Joe Namath and Babe Parilli; Colts — Earl Morrall and Johnny Unitas

---

Sec. 07

Row 19

Seat 12

Enter
Gate C
Upper Tier

"That's the difference between this year and last year. This year, he has a funny interpreter."

–Yankees shortstop Derek Jeter, after pitcher Hideki Irabu laughed at a joke when it was translated

FULL SEASON TICKET

THE SHORT END
OF THE STICK

1. In what World Series did the Yankees outscore their opponent, 55-27, and still lose the Series?

2. The Jets lost the infamous "Heidi Game" to what team?

3. The Yankees lost the "Pine Tar Game" to what team?

4. On March 2, 1962, the Knicks lost to the Philadelphia Warriors at Hershey, PA. What is this game best known for?

5. The New York Mets have lost only one World Series. To whom?

6. In 1961 and '62, the Giants lost NFL Championship Games to the same team. Which one?

7. Since 1960, the Rangers have lost in the Stanley Cup Finals two times. To what teams?

8. Who was the losing pitcher in the last game of the 1951 Giant-Dodger playoffs?

9. Since 1960, the Knicks have lost in the NBA Finals three times. To what teams?

10. For experts only: When the Yankees completed the "Pine Tar Game" weeks later, they put a future Cy Young winner in center field and a future MVP at second base. Name both of these lefties.

ANSWERS

1. The 1960 Series against the Pirates

2. Oakland Raiders

3. Kansas City Royals

4. Wilt Chamberlain scored 100 points in the game.

5. The Oakland A's (1973)

6. Green Bay Packers

7. Boston (1972) and Montreal (1979)

8. Ralph Branca — In fact, he was the pitcher of record in both Dodger losses in that playoff.

9. LA Lakers (1972), Houston Rockets (1994) and San Antonio Spurs (1999)

10. Center field — Ron Guidry and second base — Don Mattingly

"Wimbledon is perfect to play tennis in, while Flushing Meadows is just the opposite, like playing in an airport."

–Mats Wilander

Sec. 16

Row 51

Seat 7a

Enter Gate G

Lower Tier

POLO GROUNDS POSERS

Let's bring you back to the days of (and even before) Willie, Mickey and the Duke. We're talkin' baseball and we're talkin' the New York Giants.

1. In which borough did the Giants play their home games?

2. What man managed the Giants to ten pennants?

3. What Giant was the last National Leaguer to hit .400? (Hint: His initials are B.T.)

4. Who pitched three shutouts in six days for the Giants in the 1905 World Series? He won 372 games for the Giants during his career.

5. What Giant won 24 straight decisions?

6. Who was the Giant primary catcher on their last two pennant-winning teams? (Hint: He later managed the Mets and the San Francisco Giants.)

7. What two Giants hit 50 HRs in a season?

8. By how many games did the Giants win the pennant in 1951?

9. In what year did the NY Giants win their last World Series? Who were their opponents?

10. For experts only: What player (and later Giant manager) hit the most home runs in NYC?

ANSWERS

1. Manhattan
2. John McGraw
3. Bill Terry hit .401 in 1930.
4. Christy Mathewson
5. Carl Hubbell
6. Wes Westrum
7. Willie Mays and Johnny Mize
8. One
9. In 1954 they swept the Cleveland Indians.
10. Mel Ott (323)

Sec. 82 Row E Seat 17

Enter Gate B

"Everyone has some fear. A man who
has no fear belongs in a mental hospital.
Or on special teams."

–Jets coach Walt Michaels

RED STORM - INITIALLY SPEAKING

Below are the initials of St. Johns players who were NBA first round picks. The year and team that drafted each is provided. How many do you know?

1. D.M. — 1949 — Knicks
2. S.D. — 1967 — Pistons and Nets
3. B.W. — 1985 — Mavericks
4. C.M. — 1985 — Warriors
5. W.B. — 1986 — Trailblazers
6. M.J. — 1987 — Knicks
7. J.W. — 1990 — Suns
8. M.S. — 1992 — Pacers
9. F.L. — 1998 — Spurs
10. R.A. — 1999 — Bulls

ANSWERS

1. Dick McGuire
2. Sonny Dove
3. Bill Wennington
4. Chris Mullin
5. Walter Berry
6. Mark Jackson
7. Jayson Williams
8. Malik Sealy
9. Felipe Lopez
10. Ron Artest

Sec.	Row	Seat	Enter Gate B
82	E	17	

"Reggie (Jackson) would give you the shirt off his back. Of course, he'd call a press conference to announce it."

–Yankees pitcher Jim "Catfish" Hunter

THE YANKES -
FOR THE RECORD

1. Only two players have hit three home runs in a World Series game. Name them.

2. Only one player has caught a perfect World Series game. Who?

3. Who is the only manager to win five straight World Series?

4. In 1986, this Yankee captain had a Yankee-record 238 hits in a season along with a .352 batting average and 53 doubles. Who is he?

5. Who holds the AL record for RBIs in a season?

6. What Yankee led the league in stolen bases in 1988?

7. Name two of the four Yankee Cy Young Award winners.

8. Who holds the major league consecutive game hitting streak record? What is it?

9. Who hit six grand slams in 1987 and also homered in eight straight games?

10. For experts only: Since 1960, only two Yankee pitchers have won 20 games in back-to-back seasons. Can you think of one of them?

ANSWERS

1. Babe Ruth (twice) and Reggie Jackson

2. Yogi Berra

3. Casey Stengel (1949-'53)

4. Don Mattingly

5. Lou Gehrig (184)

6. Rickey Henderson had a Yankee-record 93 in 1988.

7. Bob Turley (1958), Whitey Ford (1961), Sparky Lyle (1977) and Ron Guidry (1978)

8. Joe DiMaggio, 56

9. Don Mattingly

10. Mel Stottlemyre (1968 and '69) and Tommy John (1979 and '80)

"Pro football is like nuclear warfare. There are no winners, only survivors."

–Frank Gifford

Sec. 16

Row 51

Seat 7a

Enter Gate G

Lower Tier

COLLEGE EXAMS

What are the nicknames of the following seven New York colleges sports teams?

1. Army
2. Columbia
3. Fordham
4. Iona
5. Manhattan
6. St. Johns
7. Syracuse
8. Which one of the above colleges won a Sugar Bowl?
9. Which one of the above colleges won a Rose Bowl?
10. For experts only: One of the above colleges had three Heisman Trophy winners. Which school and what players?

FULL SEASON

Sec. 17
Row K
Seat 22
Gate F

**"When you win, you're an old pro.
When you lose, you're an old man."**

–Giants quarterback Charlie Conerly

ANSWERS

1. Black Knights

2. Lions

3. Rams

4. Gaels

5. Jaspers

6. Red Storm

7. Orangemen

8. Fordham shut out Missouri, 2-0, in 1942.

9. Columbia blanked Stanford, 7-0, in 1934.

10. Army — Doc Blanchard (1945), Glenn Davis (1946) and Pete Dawkins (1958)

Sec. 07

Row 19

Seat 12

Enter
Gate C
Upper Tier

**"If we didn't have a huddle,
Jim would have no social life."**

*–Giants quarterback Phil Simms, about his
teammate Jim Burt*

FULL SEASON TICKET

1962
AN AMAZIN' YEAR

The National League returned to NYC in 1962 when the Amazin' Mets began play. The following questions refer to that team.

1. They played 160 games. Within five, how many games did they win?

2. Who was their manager?

3. Their lead-off hitter is in the Hall of Fame. Name him.

4. Name one of their pitchers who lost 20 games.

5. The man who hit the first Met home run later became a Met manager. Who is he?

6. What former Yankee hit 16 home runs for the Mets, while leading the league's first basemen in errors?

7. The Met left fielder that year hit 34 home runs. Who?

8. What other expansion team entered the NL that year?

9. In what stadium did the Mets play their home games?

10. For experts only: The Mets Opening Day third baseman suffered through a 0 for 34 streak and was eventually traded to Cincinnati. Name this man who managed 13 years in the majors.

ANSWERS

1. 40 — They finished 40-120.
2. Casey Stengel
3. Richie Ashburn
4. Roger Craig (24) and Al Jackson (20)
5. Gil Hodges
6. Marv Throneberry
7. Frank Thomas
8. Houston Colt .45s (later renamed the Astros)
9. The Polo Grounds
10. Don Zimmer

Sec.	Row	Seat		
82	E	17	Enter Gate B	

"**The New York Rangers are celebrating their victory by traveling around the city carrying the Stanley Cup. And out of habit, many New Yorkers are throwing change in it.**"

-TV talk show host Conan O'Brien

ODDLY ENOUGH

1. What pitcher started Game 1 of the 1976 World Series *against* the Yankees and Game 1 of the '77 Series *for* the Yankees?

2. Why, in the past, did the NY Rangers play some of their home playoff games in Toronto?

3. How many different times did Billy Martin manage the Yankees?

4. True or false? Two Yankees who pitched perfect games went to the same high school.

5. What Olympic decathlon winner played outfield for the NY Giants?

6. The major league record for consecutive losses by a pitcher is 27. What young Met experienced this agony of defeat?

7. True or false? A five-year-old thoroughbred won a Triple Crown race in New York.

8. What team did the Giants beat in an NFC championship game without scoring a touchdown?

9. What movie was the cause of Walt Frazier's nickname?

10. For experts only: When Ron Guidry won the Cy Young Award in 1978, he had only three losses — each to a pitcher with the first name "Mike." Guidry's last victory that year was also against a pitcher named "Mike." The mike is all yours, if you can come up with any of them.

ANSWERS

1. Don Gullett

2. When the circus came to Madison Square Garden, the Rangers had to leave.

3. Five

4. True — Don Larsen and David Wells both attended Point Loma High School in San Diego.

5. Jim Thorpe

6. Anthony Young, in 1992 and '93

7. True — In 1890, five-year-old Montague won the Preakness (yes, the Preakness!) in New York.

8. The 49ers, in 1990 — The Giants booted five field goals to beat them, 15-13.

9. *Bonnie and Clyde* — Frazier's fashion reminded people of the way Warren Beatty dressed as Clyde Barrow in the movie, so people started calling him Clyde.

10. The losses were to Mike Caldwell, Mike Flanagan and Mike Willis. Guidry beat Mike Torrez for his last win (in the 1978 playoff game against the Red Sox).

METS MUSINGS

1. How many World Series have they participated in?

2. Can you come up with the years and their opponents in the World Series?

3. In what stadiums have they played their home games?

4. True or false? They won a World Series before winning an Opening Day Game.

5. Who was the Mets only playing manager?

6. Name the first year the Mets had a .500 record during a season.

7. Who has pitched the most Opening Day games for the Mets?

8. In 1983, what Met pinch-hit a major league record 81 times?

9. What member of the 1962 Mets team played in the Mets first World Series?

10. For experts only: The Mets leadoff hitter in the third game of each World Series in which they have participated has led off with a home run. Name these players.

"There are only two places in this league: first place and no place."

–Mets pitcher Tom Seaver

Sec. 16

Row 51

Seat 7a

Enter Gate G
Lower Tier

ANSWERS

1. Three

2. 1969 — Baltimore, 1973 — Oakland and 1986 — Boston

3. Polo Grounds and Shea Stadium

4. True

5. Joe Torre (1977)

6. 1969

7. Tom Seaver

8. Rusty Staub

9. Ed Kranepool

10. Tommie Agee (1969), Wayne Garrett (1973) and
    Lenny Dykstra (1986)

FULL SEASON | Sec. 17 Row K Seat 22 Gate F

> "Watching him pitch is like a struggling artist
> watching Michelangelo paint."
>
> *-Jerry Reuss, on fellow pitcher Tom Seaver*

JOE D.

1. What two nicknames does *The Baseball Encyclopedia* list for Joe DiMaggio?

2. What was his retired number?

3. Name his two brothers who played in the majors.

4. How many MVP Awards did he win?

5. What remarkable ratio do the numbers 361 to 369 represent?

6. How many Triple Crowns did he win?

7. In what year did he go on his famous 56-game hitting streak?

8. DiMaggio holds the Yankee record for home runs in a season by a right-handed batter. How many?

9. Excluding the hitting streak, there are only two career offensive categories in which DiMaggio is in the Yankee top three. Name one of the categories.

10. For experts only: What Pacific Coast League team did he play for before joining the Yankees?

Sec. 07

Row 19

Seat 12

Enter
Gate C
Upper Tier

"If I ever go to Russia and meet with Gorbachev, the news stories will start with, 'Bill Bradley, former New York Knick.'"

–Bill Bradley

FULL SEASON TICKET

ANSWERS

1. Joltin' Joe and the Yankee Clipper
2. Five
3. Dom and Vince
4. Three
5. He had 361 career home runs and only 369 career strikeouts.
6. None
7. 1941
8. 46
9. Triples and RBIs
10. San Francisco Seals

Sec. 82 · Row E · Seat 17 · Enter Gate B

"New Yorkers love it when you spill your guts out there. You spill your guts out at Wimbledon, they make you stop and clean it up."

–Tennis star Jimmy Connors, on the U.S. Open

DEVILISH QUESTIONS

1. The Devils franchise did not originate in New Jersey. Do you know their two previous homes?

2. Who was their goalie in their first game played in New Jersey?

3. After a 13-4 loss to Edmonton in 1983, what Disney character did Wayne Gretzky liken the Devil franchise to?

4. What Devil won the Rookie of the Year Award?

5. In what year did the Devils win the Stanley Cup?

6. What Norris Trophy winner was the Devils captain of their Stanley Cup winning team?

7. Name the coach and name the general manager when they won the Cup.

8. What Devil won the Conn Smythe Award as MVP of the playoffs?

9. What team did the Devils sweep in the finals to win the Cup?

10. For experts only: What Swede (who had a twin who also played for the Devils) scored an NHL-record eight points in a playoff game?

ANSWERS

1. They were the Kansas City Scouts from 1974-'76 and the Colorado Rockies from 1976-'82.

2. Chico Resch

3. Mickey Mouse

4. Martin Brodeur, in 1994

5. 1995

6. Scott Stevens

7. Coach — Jacques Lemaire and General Manager — Lou Lamoriello

8. Claude Lemieux

9. Detroit Red Wings

10. Patrik Sundstrom had three goals and five assists against Washington in a 1988 playoff game.

"There are close to 11 million unemployed and half of them are New York Yankee managers."

–Former Tonite Show *host Johnny Carson*

| Sec. 16 |
| Row 51 |
| Seat 7a |
| Enter Gate G |
| Lower Tier |

HODGEPODGE

1. What Manhattan school lost the 1945 NCAA Championship basketball game?

2. What governor of New York played minor league baseball for the Pittsburgh Pirates?

3. What player did the Knicks trade to get Charles Oakley and whom did they get when they traded Oak years later?

4. What "moose" hit the only seventh-game World Series grand slam?

5. Name Herschel Walker's first pro football team.

6. In the 1965 draft, the Knicks third-round pick was the identical twin of the Pistons third-round pick. Both brothers played a dozen years and ended their careers playing together with Phoenix. Name them.

7. What coach with more than 700 NCAA basketball victories coached Army from 1966-'71?

8. The Giants played in the NFL's first overtime game. Against what team? Did they win or lose?

9. Rich Kotite was head coach of the Jets for two seasons. How many games did the team win during that time?

10. For experts only: What special event occurred at the first major league night game played in Brooklyn?

ANSWERS

1. NYU lost to Oklahoma A & M.

2. Mario Cuomo

3. They traded Bill Cartwright and got Marcus Camby.

4. Bill "Moose" Skowron, in the 1956 Series

5. New Jersey Generals of the USFL

6. Dick and Tom Van Arsdale — Dick played for the Knicks.

7. Bobby Knight

8. They lost the 1958 NFL Championship Game to the Johnny Unitas-led Baltimore Colts.

9. Four — They lost 28.

10. Johnny Vander Meer pitched his second consecutive no-hitter.

FULL SEASON

Sec. 17
Row K
Seat 22
Gate F

"I skate to where the puck is going to be, not where it has been."

–Wayne Gretzky

ON THE AIR

Below are descriptions of New York sports announcers.
Identify them from the clues.

1. They were the Mets three original television announcers
   in 1962.

2. She was the first female broadcaster to announce a Yankee
   game.

3. This 300-game winner announced for both the Mets and
   Yankees.

4. He and his son both did radio play-by-play for the Rangers.

5. No other sports announcer has used the word "cannoli" on the
   air more than he has.

6. This long-time Yankee announcer's signature phrase was:
   "How about that?"

7. Later, he became the National League president.

8. He's a lickety-quick Knick rhymester.

9. He caught in four decades.

10. For experts only: What announcer is known for the call,
    "The Giants win the pennant; the Giants win the pennant;
    the Giants win the pennant; ..."?

ANSWERS

1. Ralph Kiner, Bob Murphy and Lindsey Nelson
2. Suzyn Waldman
3. Tom Seaver
4. Marv and Kenny Albert
5. Phil Rizzuto
6. Mel Allen
7. Bill White
8. Walt Frazier
9. Tim McCarver
10. Russ Hodges

Sec. 07
Row 19
Seat 12
Enter
Gate C
Upper Tier

"I get up at 6 a.m.
no matter what time it is."

–Yogi Berra

FULL SEASON TICKET

YANKEE DOODLE DANDY

1. Name the Yankee Triple Crown winners.

2. In 1984, what Yankees finished one-two in batting average in the league?

3. The first Puerto Rican to win 20 games in a season in the majors did so for the Yankees in 1978. Can you name him? (Hint: His last name contains each of the five vowels.)

4. In that 1978 season, what Yankee pitcher went 25-3?

5. Who made the last out in that pitcher's 25th victory?

6. Only one time have hitters from the same team finished 1-2-3 in home runs. Can you name them?

7. What Yankee manager was the first batter ever for the Kansas City Royals? (Hint: That year (1969) he was the league's Rookie of the Year.)

8. What head coach with more than 300 NFL wins played 12 games for the Yankees in 1919?

9. What Yankee in 1981 had a 0.77 ERA for the year, striking out better than one batter per inning?

10. For experts only: Six Yankees have hit home runs from both sides of the plate in the same game. How many can you name?

ANSWERS

1. Mickey Mantle and Lou Gehrig
2. Don Mattingly edged out Dave Winfield for the batting title.
3. Ed Figueroa
4. Ron Guidry
5. Carl Yastrzemski
6. Babe Ruth (60), Lou Gehrig (47) and Tony Lazzeri (18) did this in 1927.
7. Lou Piniella
8. George Halas
9. Goose Gossage
10. Mickey Mantle, Tom Tresh, Roy White, Roy Smalley, Bernie Williams and Jorge Posada

FULL SEASON	Sec. 17 Row K Seat 22 Gate F	"I come from the Lower East Side, where the only guys with rackets are hoodlums."
		–Comedian Alan King, on tennis

KNICK-KNACKS

Name the Knick who:

1. Led the league in scoring.

2. Won the Heisman Trophy.

3. Was NBA Rookie of the Year.

4. Won the Sixth Man Award.

5. Led the league in assists and steals in 1978-'79 and 1979-'80.

6. Was the NBA's first lottery pick.

7. Knick coach who was a Knick first-round draft pick

8. Knick coach who later coached an NCAA Championship team

9. Won Coach of the Year Award.

10. For experts only: Name three of the four Knicks who were first-team All-Stars.

Sec. 82 E Row 17 Seat Enter Gate B

"If they took away our sticks and gave us brooms, we'd still have fights."

-Rangers center Phil Esposito

ANSWERS

1. Bernard King (1984-'85)

2. Charlie Ward

3. Willis Reed (1965), Patrick Ewing (1986) and Mark Jackson (1988)

4. John Starks (1997)

5. Micheal Ray Richardson

6. Patrick Ewing (1984)

7. Dick McGuire

8. Rick Pitino — The NCAA title was with Kentucky.

9. Red Holzman (1970) and Pat Riley (1993)

10. Harry Gallatin (1954), Willis Reed (1970), Walt Frazier (1970, '72, '74, '75) and Bernard King (1984, '85)

"I won't be active in the day-to-day operations of the club at all. I'll stick to ships."

–George Steinbrenner, after buying the Yankees in 1973

| Sec. 16 |
| Row 51 |
| Seat 7a |
| Enter Gate G |
| Lower Tier |

HOMETOWN HEROES

Each of the following is a native of New York City. How many can you identify?

1. He has scored the most NBA points.

2. He started with the Mets in 1962 and played his entire 18-year career with them.

3. He is the New Yorker with the most major league home runs.

4. He's the only player to lead the NBA in scoring and assists in the same year.

5. He's the major league pitcher who won the most games in his last season.

6. This MVP's nickname is the Scooter.

7. He's the only New Yorker who scored more than 500 NHL goals.

8. This pitcher has won and lost the most World Series games.

9. His retired number is 613.

10. For experts only: He led the American League in home runs in 1959 with the Indians and, in 1968, won a game as a pitcher with the Yankees.

ANSWERS

1. Kareem Abdul-Jabbar
2. Ed Kranepool
3. Lou Gehrig
4. Nate "Tiny" Archibald
5. Sandy Koufax (27)
6. Phil Rizzuto
7. Joey Mullen
8. Whitey Ford
9. Red Holzman
10. Rocky Colavito

Sec. 07

Row 19

Seat 12

Enter
Gate C
Upper Tier

"That picture was taken out of context."

*–Mets pitcher Jeff Innis, complaining about
a bad newspaper photo of him*

FULL SEASON TICKET

THE YANKS - HISTORY IN THE MAKING

1. When the American League started in 1901, New York didn't have a franchise. One of the other American League teams moved to NY in 1903. Where did this team come from?

2. What was the first name of the NY American League team?

3. What current hospital is located on the site of the first stadium (Hilltop Park) which the NY American League team used (from 1903-1912)?

4. What team traded Babe Ruth to the Yankees?

5. Who was the first Yankee to lead the league in home runs? (Hint: He has four letters in his last name and three of them are the same.)

6. In 1913, what stadium did the Yankees move to?

7. In 1923, the Yankees moved to Yankee Stadium. What famed bandmaster led a march to center field to raise the 1922 AL pennant?

8. Who hit the first home run in Yankee Stadium?

9. What future Yankee manager hit the first World Series home run in Yankee Stadium?

10. For experts only: Who was the winning pitcher for New York in their first home game? (Hint: He won 41 games for the Yankees in 1904.)

ANSWERS

1. Baltimore — They were the Baltimore Orioles.

2. The Highlanders

3. Columbia Presbyterian Hospital

4. Boston Red Sox

5. Wally Pipp led the AL in 1916 and '17.

6. The Polo Grounds, which they shared with the Giants for ten years

7. John Phillip Sousa

8. Babe Ruth

9. Casey Stengel of the Giants, in 1923

10. Jack Chesbro defeated Washington, 6-2, on April 20, 1903.

Sec.	Row	Seat
82	E	17

Enter Gate B

"**Baseball players are smarter than football players. How often do you see a baseball team penalized for too many men on the field?**"

–Yankees pitcher Jim Bouton

THE GIANTS — SIMPLY SUPER

1. Name the Giants two opponents in the Super Bowl.

2. Who were the Giants starting quarterbacks in both games?

3. How about the starting quarterbacks for their opponents?

4. What were the locations of these games?

5. In their first Super Bowl, the Giant quarterback attempted 25 passes. How many were complete?

6. Four Giants have caught Super Bowl TD passes. How many do you know?

7. What Giant ran for two touchdowns in one of these games?

8. What player was the Giants leading rusher in their first Super Bowl?

9. Who missed a 47-yard field goal to enable the Giants to win their second Super Bowl?

10. For experts only: There was a safety in each of these two Super Bowl games. Can you name the players credited with these safeties? (Hint: One was a Giant; the other wasn't.)

ANSWERS

1. Denver Broncos — XXI and Buffalo Bills — XXV

2. Phil Simms — XXI and Jeff Hostetler — XXV

3. XXI-Denver — John Elway and XXV-Buffalo — Jim Kelly

4. The first was held in Pasadena and the second in Tampa.

5. Simms completed 22 of 25 for a record 88% completion ratio.

6. XXI — Mark Bravaro, Phil McConkey and Zeke Mowatt; XXV — Stephen Baker

7. Ottis Anderson

8. Joe Morris, with 67 yards

9. Scott Norwood (or, as he is sometimes called in Buffalo, Scott "Norwide")

10. XXI — George Martin and XXV — Bruce Smith

"Don't blame me. Blame the foursome ahead of me."

-Giants linebacker Lawrence Taylor, after being late for practice

| Sec. 16 |
| Row 51 |
| Seat 7a |

Enter Gate G
Lower Tier

LAST DANCE

The following players were known primarily for playing with New York teams but actually ended their careers with other cities. Match the player with the city.

1. Walt Frazier
2. Eddie Giacomin
3. Sam Huff
4. Jerry Koosman
5. Joe Namath
6. Graig Nettles
7. Tom Seaver
8. Duke Snider
9. Bryan Trottier
10. Mookie Wilson

a) Boston
b) Cleveland
c) Detroit
d) Los Angeles
e) Montreal
f) Philadelphia
g) Pittsburgh
h) San Francisco
i) Toronto
j) Washington

FULL SEASON

Sec. 17
Row K
Seat 22
Gate F

"Whitey (Ford) and I figured out once that each year I hit about fifteen long outs at Yankee Stadium that would have been home runs at Ebbets Field. In my eighteen years I would have gotten 270 additional home runs if I'd been a Dodger."

–*Mickey Mantle*

ANSWERS

1. B
2. C
3. J
4. F
5. D
6. E
7. A
8. H
9. G
10. I

Sec. 07

Row 19

Seat 12

Enter
Gate C

Upper Tier

"Each time it's like being in a head-on car accident."

–Jets running back Matt Snell, about carrying the ball

FULL SEASON TICKET